"Kathi offers wisdom about how to live through tough personal challenges, but even more she offers a spirit of joy about how these challenges can enrich life. Her story and her insights are an inspiration to all of us who live in this all-too-often-difficult world."

Pastor Michelle Abbott,
Oak Knoll Lutheran Church

"Meeting Kathi for the first time, it was notable to me how bright her spirit was in spite of her disability. She greeted me with a warm smile, a smile that continued to shine in all of our encounters. It was only a short time before she was right at home among the people, a tribute to her undying hope that God works for good in all things with those who love Him."

Pastor Paul Pettersen,
Normandale Community Church

"Kathi Holmes' story is just one of many that affirm Courage Center's mission "to empower people with disabilities to realize their full potential in every aspect of life." Recovering from an illness or injury is hard work, but as Kathi proves, persistence, hard work and professionals like those who work at Courage Center can produce amazing results."

Susan Warner, Courage Center

"I Stand With Courage" is definitely an inspiring story, and I could certainly relate to much of what Kathi went through. Her courage and determination are amazing, and she is living proof that people can become "bitter or better" when faced with life's challenges. Kathi simply was not willing to take "no" for an answer when it came to her paralysis!"

Meg Corrigan, author of *Then I Am Strong:
Moving From My Mother's Daughter to God's Child.*

I Stand With Courage

One Woman's Journey to Conquer Paralysis

Kathryn M. Holmes

Inspiring Voices®
A Service of **Guideposts**

Original images created by Miles Sieloff
Author photo by Nancy Chakrin

Inspiring Voices books may be ordered
through booksellers or by contacting:

Inspiring Voices
1663 Liberty Drive
Bloomington, IN 47403
www.inspiringvoices.com
1-(866) 697-5313

ISBN: 978-1-4624-0022-5 (sc)
ISBN: 978-1-4624-0021-8 (e)

Library of Congress Control Number: 2011940252

Printed in the United States of America

Inspiring Voices rev. date: 10/27/2011

Contents

Dedication

Blessings to my husband Charlie, daughter Paula and son-in-law Chris, son Miles, all our friends who traveled this journey with us, and my granddaughter Olivia who inspired my courage.

And to all those who are facing an uphill health battle—keep fighting, be determined, and keep God on your side.

Acknowledgments

To my husband, Charlie, who traveled with me while on his own health journey and patiently responded to a plethora of my questions related to creating this book.

To my son, Miles, who encouraged and supported me and took time out of his busy graduate school schedule to draw illustrations for the book.

To my daughter, Paula, who was my rock, my caregiver when I needed it, and who never let me forget to keep striving for mobility.

To all the doctors, nurses, physical therapists, home health aides, and other caring people in health care that took care of me—and cared for me.

To Courage Center—without them, I likely would be paralyzed. What a gift.

To my editor and publishing guide extraordinaire, Connie Anderson of Words & Deeds, Inc.

To the Women of Words group for their input on naming of the book, especially Meg Corrigan, Caryn Sullivan, and Betty Liedtke for reading the book and offering valuable comments to enhance it.

To my friend and proofreader, Pat Spilseth, Writer's Circle, for leading me back on the path to writing and to thinking outside the box.

To author and friend, Sandra Humphrey, for her inspiration and guidance.

To Inspiring Voices, my publisher, for this venture.

To Pastor Paul and Pastor Michelle for their encouragement and the people of Oak Knoll Lutheran Church, who made us believe we might truly be a miracle.

And especially to God for giving me the courage and determination to overcome my handicap and blessing Charlie and me with His healing power.

Introduction

In the spring of 1988 I had a blind date with the man who would become my future husband. A mutual friend passed along my telephone number to Charlie. He called, and we met for a pleasant dinner at a local restaurant. Divorced for seven years, I had met more than enough undesirables. As we talked, I realized we had different interests. Charlie enjoyed opera; I liked to listen to jazz. His style was more traditional; mine more modern. He had traveled extensively in the Navy while I sailed only the local lakes. Still I enjoyed his company, and we shared common values. In fact, the longer we knew each other, the more comfortable we were together.

Neither of us was athletic; however, we liked to keep active. We signed up for charity walks through our respective employers. Side by side we walked and talked. After his fiftieth birthday, Charlie decided to train for the Twin Cities Marathon. In 1990 he completed the marathon. The following summer he signed up for Grandma's Marathon along Lake Superior's North Shore. Stopping at various points along the routes, I cheered him to the finish.

Charlie and I both were raised only children. Even though he had been married before, he did not have children. My two children, Paula and Miles, were just entering their thorny teenage years. He admitted that the stress of teenagers could have been a deal breaker. Nevertheless, he took the leap and we married in 1992. Charlie was always more level-headed and rational than I was. He knew enough to let me be the disciplinarian, but gave me his full support.

We were a team. We biked together and exercised at the YMCA—he in the gym and I swam in the pool. We survived the turbulent teenage years, and when Paula and Miles moved out, we moved into a condo. Charlie retired first and often had meals waiting for me when I came home from work. Soon after he retired, I entered semi-retirement due to cutbacks.

Our life was uncomplicated, relaxed, and satisfying.

**"O afflicted one,
lashed by storms,
and not comforted,
I will rebuild you ..."**
Isaiah 54:11 (NIV)

I

Stormy Weather

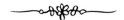

Signs had been everywhere; nevertheless, it wasn't until the beginning of 2008 that the world began to hear rumblings in the media about the instability of the financial market. As the year progressed, the financial time bomb continued to tick louder. September 2008 the banking industry collapsed. Headlines were plastered around the world. This began a progression of bailouts, layoffs, and foreclosures.

Similarly, Charlie and my personal lives, prior to 2008, were stable and peaceful. However, like the economy, we had early signs of future health problems.

As the country began experiencing the financial crisis, ominous clouds were sweeping over our world as well. Like a tornado, the sudden swell of power and force left destruction in its wake.

Our world as we had known it was altered forever.

This is our journey.

In April of 2008, Charlie had just finished teaching a driver's safety class. He was bending over a drinking fountain, lost his balance, and fell. Paramedics whisked him to the hospital to repair a broken femur in the upper leg. He was left hobbling with a walker for several months.

A month after Charlie's accident, I was having symptoms of an upper respiratory infection which was not responding to antibiotics. With my history of the autoimmune disease, microscopic polyangiitus, I was referred to a rheumatologist. With a straightforward demeanor, he reviewed my lab results and calmly said, "Kathryn, your autoimmune disease has returned. Once again we need to put you on Prednisone and schedule six months of chemotherapy treatments. Having had this before you know this is the only way we can suppress your immune system enough to shake this disease. Because oral corticosteroids such as Prednisone affect the entire body, instead of one particular area, it is most likely to cause significant side effects. At the high levels I'm prescribing, you may experience increased blood pressure and high blood sugar, which can trigger the onset of diabetes. You need to keep your distance from sick people, as you will be subjected to an increased risk of infections."

"Yes, I know." I replied. "And I remember the weight gain, with fat deposits around my stomach and face. After several months I looked like a blowfish!"

"We can do nothing about that because the combination of Prednisone and Cytoxan is the only way we know to stabilize your immune system. It is overacting and killing all cells, including the healthy ones, especially in your lungs and kidneys."

"Well, I've gone through this treatment before and survived. I can handle another go-around," I said confidently.

"You need to keep track of any bruising or injuries that do not seem to heal. We will watch for bone fractures or the onset of osteoporosis. Should we see these conditions coming, I'll put you on an osteoporosis drug to prevent bone breakdown and increase bone density. Do you have any questions?"

"No, but I never thought I would get this back again."

Meanwhile, Charlie's leg was healing but he was getting weaker, forcing more trips to the emergency room. An angiogram revealed he needed a quadruple heart bypass. That was in July.

By August, I was exhausted, not recovering as I had during the first bout with this same autoimmune disease. Once in September and twice in October, Charlie dropped me off at the hospital emergency room door where I was met by a volunteer who helped me into a wheelchair. Charlie was too weak to help me get out of the car or to walk from the hospital parking ramp to the emergency area. He was forced to leave me there alone. The x-rays from each of these visits showed I suffered a fractured vertebra. I needed bone repair.

Charlie admitted that he, too, was wearing down. He confessed, "I don't feel well. I haven't gotten my stamina back from the open-heart surgery." Having observed his slow gait and fatigue, I nodded with understanding. Worst of all, Charlie and I had reached a place where, after twenty years together, we were powerless to help each other.

The first to ask, "What's for dinner?" had to make it: we barely had the energy to pop a dinner into the microwave. Most of the day I dozed in a recliner. I only got up to use the bathroom. My body melted into that chair. It held me captive for hours on end.

On the evening of November 1, as I stood in my bedroom doorway getting ready to dress for bed, my legs collapsed. My body was in free fall. I grasped for the doorframe, a chair, anything as I avalanched to the floor, landing in a heap. Fear grabbed at my stomach when I could not get up. After my husband's frantic 911 call, paramedics arrived and carted me away, leaving my ailing husband behind.

All the signs had been there, but I was still blindsided when my body gave way.

II

Shock and Helplessness

The shock, the disease, and the pain medication left me vulnerable and confused. All I thought was, *I am as helpless as a turtle turned over on its shell.* My entire body was weak; my mind was scrambled.

When I was admitted to the hospital, my first room was in the hospice section. *What has happened to me? Am I going to die?* My thoughts reeled to the worst possible scenarios. Compassionate nurses assured me I was in the hospice section because no other beds were available—and for no other reason. In hospice, they spoiled me with warm blankets and handmade quilts, turning me regularly from side to side as my lower body was limp and numb. They fluffed my pillows and checked on me often. No one seemed to have a handle on my condition. I asked, "Why can't I move?"

The nurses responded, "I'll check with the doctor." Yet, no doctor arrived.

A day and a half of wondering and worrying went by. Finally, a handsome, well-dressed man swaggered into my room. His eyes peered onto the clipboard without even noticing me, making no eye contact. He introduced himself as the chief of neurosurgery. Standing at the foot of my bed, he announced, "Your spine was damaged. You are paralyzed from the waist down. There is nothing that can be done." Delivering the news as if he were a bike messenger, rather than a healing physician, he turned and walked out.

I was devastated, stunned, and so enraged I could not speak. I felt like I had been dropped down the rabbit hole in *Alice in Wonderland*. I was entering a strange and frightful world about which Alice never could have dreamed.

The next day a hospital-assigned doctor came in. Still angry, I hoped for relief from my confusion and hopelessness. She frightened me even further when she said, "We are ready to discharge you."

Discharged!

Not only was I unable to walk, I could not turn myself or sit up in bed without help. Both livid and terrified at what might lie ahead, I froze in shock. Noticing my alarm, the doctor stated, "A social worker will come and talk to you, explaining your options."

No social worker ever came.

My health history had been anything but ordinary. It first started when my thyroid stopped working and nearly put me in a coma. I had survived early-detected breast cancer with a lumpectomy, faced two pulmonary embolisms that could have taken my life as quickly as a strike of a match, and suffered a previous fight with this near-fatal autoimmune disease, microscopic polyangiitus.

This uncommon disease, with the strange name, affected the small- and medium-sized blood vessels leaving me with kidney and lung deficiencies. Any one of these conditions could have ended my life, but they didn't.

I had already survived many challenges. Growing up in a chaotic home, I had to learn to overcome the ranting, raving, and verbal abuse of an alcoholic father. My first marriage ended in divorce, and I found myself raising two children alone. One year, the day after Christmas, I arrived at work and found my desk cleared: I was out of a job. With holiday bills looming and the job market slow, I partnered with another company: together we started a new recruitment advertising agency. My health history and my background made me stronger, all adding fuel to my confidence. I was born into a Scandinavian family with strong, female role models: I believed the words to the popular songs, "I Am Woman" and "I Will Survive."

Always a fighter and a survivor, I was too weak to overcome this blow. But I was *not* too frail to insist they transfer me to the Mayo Clinic in Rochester, Minnesota for a second evaluation. "I need to have some answers. I can't just walk out and resume my life," I asserted emphatically.

"We don't refer patients to the Mayo Clinic," the doctor said, ignoring my frantic tone. Lost and fighting desperately for my life, I demanded, "I want to go to the Mayo Clinic!"

"Transferring you there is not a simple process," the doctor retorted. "It's complicated; it takes a referral."

By now I was fuming. On the verge of tears, I was determined they not set me out, adrift and alone, without knowing the complications of my condition—and what lie ahead.

"I already called them and have a patient number," I countered. This was true; however, it had been several months since I had been in contact with the Mayo Clinic's intake person. "Give me the phone, and I will call them," I added. I angrily thought, *Why do I have to plead my case? They are dismissing me without considering my current condition or my complicated health history. I don't trust these doctors. They aren't concerned about my well-being.*

The doctor left my room. Less than an hour later, she returned with the news. "We will be transferring you to the Mayo Clinic tomorrow."

I learned a lot can be done if you press hard enough.

Dressed elegantly in a faded, open-back hospital gown, and covered by a thin blanket, I was lifted onto a transport bed. Assistants wheeled me out into the biting Minnesota cold and slid me into a warm van that would take me to the Mayo Clinic, nearly one hundred miles away. I slept for most of the hour and a half ride to Rochester.

After being wiggled and jiggled into a bed at the Mayo Clinic, I was asked questions I could not answer. Foggy from painkillers and numbed by disbelief, I barely knew my name. The pain, paralysis, and confusion left me exhausted. My body was cold, my mind numb; I was disconnected from my feelings.

A team of doctors, each with different specialties, woke me and introduced themselves. I remember staring deep into the wise, blue eyes of the head doctor, begging from the core of my being, "Can you help me?" This was not like me. I never asked for help. I felt despondent, as if I had fallen in a deep hole and was desperately grasping a rope to pull me out.

My daughter Paula was my rock, staying with me for several days. "Mom, I brought you some clothes. Are these the pants you wanted? Here is our family picture so you remember we are always with you. You may need this framed prayer you gave me." She was trying to comfort me, but I saw the worry and sadness in her face.

Her boyfriend Chris came with her one day. He knew how concerned Paula was about me. When she left the room, I asked him, "Would you stay with her while I am going through all this?"

He said, "I will be with her forever." That was the highlight of my day.

Paula always seeks answers. As a toddler her first words were, "What's that?" and now her word was, "Why?" An interning doctor from India, part of the seven-person medical team, took a dry erase marker to the white board in my room and showed us how the nerves in my spine had been damaged from fat deposits as a result of the heavy doses of Prednisone. I knew that one of the side effects of Prednisone was an accumulation of fat deposits around the face and abdomen; however, lodging in and thus damaging a spine was a rare occurrence. Given my health history of *rare occurrences*, I wasn't surprised. Despite several MRIs at the previous hospital, this was the first time I was told what had caused this paralysis.

The doctors talked of surgery and searched for answers to resolve the paralysis.

Considering my age, health history and the forming of osteoporosis, my family and I, as well as the doctors, all agreed surgery was far too risky. The doctors were concerned that the results of surgery may or may not relieve the paralysis. Doctors from seven different medical specialties paraded through my room daily, checking on any progress, and ensuring all my secondary health issues were addressed. All the bases were covered. I was provided diabetes instruction as the Prednisone had exacerbated my blood sugars. My lung function was being monitored, and I had oxygen tubes running into my nose. The deep concern that the doctors showed, and the fact that they were reviewing my entire medical history, made me feel appreciated and cared for.

That's all anyone wants:
To know we are cared for when we need
support the most.

III

Anger and Depression

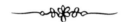

Why me? I fought these words that wanted to strangle my thoughts. I knew that God was stronger. Though I wanted to fight back, or at least bargain with Him, I knew I would be fighting a losing battle. God would do what He wanted with my life. I have always believed in God and His love. My God is not an angry god. In the movie *The Thorn Birds,* when the young priest was drowning, he opened his arms to the heavens, and with firm conviction uttered, "Thy will be done." Sticking forever in my memory, I was inspired by his commitment to leave his life in God's hands. For us mortals, *it is hard to let go.*

I can't give up, I said to myself as I lay in my hospital bed watching the snowflakes falling through the bare trees. *I am a fighter. My children still need a mother.* Because the pain medication left me too groggy to read, I slept. I drifted away from this reality that I was not ready to accept.

One by one, the seven doctors on my team would come into my room, and each one asked me to wiggle my toes. Though I saw my toe move slightly, I didn't feel it. No matter how I tried, it was the only trick I could perform.

My body was hoisted in a sling with ropes attached to a track on the ceiling. This contraption, a cross between a hammock and a swing, was used to get me into a large leather reclining chair, permitting me to become accustomed to sitting on my own. This allowed me to get into the bathroom for much treasured showers. Not being able to shower daily, I had become obsessed by the desire to let the pulsing water cloak my body.

One day, as I started to feel achy from sitting in the reclining chair, I decided to call the nurse to hoist me back into bed. The call light was still on the bed but beyond my reach. It might as well have been miles away. The door was closed, and the halls were quiet. I couldn't move. I couldn't reach the call light. I called out in panic, "Nurse." "Nurse." "Nurse!" What if I were choking or dying, and no one came to rescue me? Panic stricken, I yelled, "Help! Help! Help me!" as loud as I could. In terror, and still not hearing any voices in the hall, I shrieked, "Help! Help! Help!" After minutes that seemed like hours, a nurse finally came. Being paralyzed had left me at risk. Two responses to fear are fight or flight. I was too traumatized to fight, too weak to flee. That's when I felt the horror of my vulnerability.

For twenty years Charlie had been supportive of all my escapades. We had become soul mates, always there when one of us needed the other. Now we were on our own. He could not be my white knight and rescue me. He was fighting his own health battles in a hospital many miles away. I tried my best to maintain an optimistic attitude when I talked to him. We would compare hospital food to see who had the best lunch. We both tried; however, it was becoming harder to be in good spirits. Charlie's only birthday gift from me that year was a phone call, and a "Happy Birthday, Hon. I love you." It broke my heart that I could not be there for him when he needed me. I knew he felt the same.

Soon I discovered that sadness promotes more sadness. In my deep despair, I thought of the many family happenings I had looked forward to that would just become memories. No longer would I stand and cook meals for my family or run into the grocery store on my way back from a day of errands. I would not go shopping with my daughter or to a hockey game with my son. I could not ride my bike on our neighborhood paths or even drive to church. What had been a normal day for me was now beyond my grasp.

I worried and wondered, *Would I be a burden to Charlie, Paula and Miles?*

The reactions from my kids were predictable. When I was diagnosed with breast cancer, Paula had collected all the literature from the library on the disease before I received it from my doctor. She wanted to know exactly what was happening to my body, the procedure, and the recovery rate. My son, Miles, was more of a caretaker. He called every day to see how I was feeling, keeping abreast with my recovery process. Now they responded to our medical predicaments in the same manner. Only this time, they had two of us to worry about. This meant the intensity of their concern was dramatically increased. They tried very hard to keep calm for our benefit.

Still feeling desperate, Paula pointed out the possibility that Charlie and I were in a medical quandary because I had brought back a lava rock from the beach on the Big Island of Hawaii. According to legend the Hawaiian goddess of fire, lightening, dance and volcanoes, Pele, is passionate, volatile, and capricious. Ever since she was jilted by a lover, she became angry if anyone removed the volcanic rock. I did. It was only one rock— as a souvenir. Paula retrieved the rock from our condo and mailed it back to Hawaii. The Internet describes hundreds of stories of bad luck befalling people who removed the lava rock. I don't know if it made any difference, but in the long run we did recover and Paula felt she had helped us.

Fortunately, hospitals do not let you hang around too long. After twelve days of stabilizing my vitals, they prepared me for discharge to a rehab center. *I can't do much physically, but I've got to try and use what I have,* I told myself. I had to learn to accept and deal with the reality of my situation. I could not dwell in the past. *Was I to be confined to a bed the rest of my life?* Not if I could help it! I needed to seek solutions for becoming more mobile.

**My goal was to gather the pieces needed
to create a new life for myself.
I didn't know it then, but accepting
my paralysis was my first step toward
recovery.**

IV

Hurdles and Acceptance

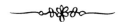

Two days before Thanksgiving—twenty-two days since my collapse—I was again lying on a transport bed in another van headed for a rehabilitation center in Minneapolis. This time I was calm and relaxed, knowing my other health issues were in check. I knew that what would happen in the future was up to me.

After the rehab center staff took my vitals, and got me settled in my room, they presented me with my rigorous schedule of daily therapy sessions.

The therapist told me to stand. I told him I couldn't. "Well, just try," he responded. As I dropped into his arms, he said, "I guess you were right." We moved on to upper-body exercises. Twice a day I came back for more. Each time I tried to push as hard as I could; all I got was hot and sweaty. The exhaustion made me vomit. Despite all the special therapy tools and equipment, they had to carry me from my wheelchair to the mat for physical therapy. Again, the physical therapists were not prepared for my full weight; they lost their grip on me. Fortunately, I landed on the mat, crumpling like a rag doll. I felt like a failure. I could not force my body to do what I wanted. I just did not have the strength to handle their therapy demands.

I realized that this Thanksgiving there would be no family-style dinner with the tasty dishes and homemade dressing. But then Miles called.

"Hi, Mom. How about I stop by the house and pick up Charlie, and we'll all have dinner together at the rehab center?"

"Wonderful idea. I'm excited already," I replied, always being brave for my kids. Charlie was temporarily out of the hospital but still needed a wheelchair. Miles wheeled him into the small, antiseptic dining room where we enjoyed the institutional salt-free meal of turkey, mashed potatoes, dressing, and pumpkin pie. At least the menu was familiar.

My mind wandered back to the usual hustle and bustle in the kitchen, while preparing all the familiar dishes and the warmth of the oven. I especially thought of the hands held around the table as we gave thanks for our food and our lives. As hard as I tried, I could not help wonder, *Would I ever experience these simple pleasures again?*

In this sterile environment, I could not capture a thankful, reflecting spirit. I thanked God that I was alive, but I could not ask Him to make me well—I felt God would give me what He wanted, no matter what I asked for. I was raised to believe it was selfish to ask God for material possessions or personal desires. My life was in His hands. Others prayed for me. *I could not.*

Twelve days after being admitted, when the aides tried to help me out of bed to go for therapy, I collapsed. The next thing I was aware of was waking in a hospital emergency room. Unfamiliar doctors were barking directions in that deliberate, yet frantic, tone that you hear in the emergency room of television medical shows. My brain was muddled. I didn't know what had happened. All I knew was I hurt.

"Stop the burning in my chest," I begged again and again. Finally my condition stabilized, and I was transferred to the cardiac unit. *Did I have a heart attack?* Ever since I had collapsed, my world had been spinning out of control. Limp and confused, I still wanted answers. "What happened to me?" The doctors first thought I had suffered a heart attack. "No, you didn't have a heart attack. You may have been given an overdose of medication which caused you to become unconscious," the doctor admitted. I was left with a question in my mind: *How could this have happened?* Unfortunately, I was too exhausted to pursue it.

The next night a nurse told me they were transferring me, my luggage, my holiday plants, and all the paraphernalia I had accumulated, to a non-cardiac floor.

The next transfer was the following evening, this time to the first floor. It seems they couldn't figure out exactly where I belonged. The evening after that, I was transferred to a larger room on the same floor. Four moves in three days. I jokingly told my family and friends they couldn't reach me because I was in the witness protection program.

My next transfer was two days later when I was transported to a long-term rehab center, where I was sent to regain my strength and to have physical therapy twice a day.

V

Threshold of a New World

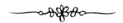

The first night at the rehab center I woke up startled and frightened in a dark room. Two muscular black men wearing surgical masks stood above me, their white eyes staring at me in the darkness. In broken English, one said, "Turn over." When I didn't respond, he firmly exclaimed, "We need to turn you now." These African men were extremely strong. With a "one, two, three," my sheet lifted, and I flipped over on my other side.

Many of the aides were from Africa. My stereotypical mindset said that everyone appearing African was from Somalia. That was certainly not the case. Realizing I knew almost nothing about Africa, I asked Charlie to bring me a map of the continent. Each time a new African-accented aide came into my room, I would ask him or her to mark his or her home on the map. They proudly wrote their initials next to their country. We shared the familiar phrase from *The Wizard of Oz,* "There's no place like home." I desperately missed my home—and they missed their homeland.

Overwhelmed and dealing with his own issues, Charlie hired a care management company to make sure I was getting quality care. Linda was a concerned advocate for me. She made sure I was given weekly showers—a hit-or-miss prospect before that time. When Linda discovered that the in-house doctor had not seen me since I was admitted two weeks prior, she checked with the nurses. Anything that did not work well, Linda was there to ensure my rights. Having this supportive advocate gave Charlie and me some relief from our medical stresses. That was money well spent.

Being this dependent on others for all my personal hygiene was most humbling. The aides answered my room call light to help me use the bedpan, prepare the lift for me to get out of bed, and assist with bathing and dressing.

As I got to know the aides, they became like family to me. Mary and Eva worked the morning shift. They were my age, with grown children and a good work ethic. Eva was a widow who had the land she owned in Greece taken from her by her family. She now worked at the rehab center and at a local department store to make ends meet. Susan and Claire had small children, and I enjoyed hearing about their kids. Jenny was planning a destination wedding. The aides' stories took me outside of the rehab walls, back into the *real* world.

Physical and occupational therapy occupied a small portion of my otherwise monotonous days. The high level of effort it took to be transferred from the bed to my wheelchair for therapy was often enough to make me hot and nauseated. Worst of all, I was totally dependent on those around me.

One day two female aides got into a tennis match of words regarding men. Shauna, the colorfully dressed, heavily built and vocally expressive one, exclaimed, "I haven't met a good man yet. I know because I've had to raise four kids and a grandbaby alone." The less flamboyant more serene woman, Linnae, had more hope for a good male relationship and tried to convince Shauna otherwise. They bickered back and forth, tossing me from one side to the other while making my bed. Though they had very different personalities, they had been best friends for years.

I began to laugh at their exaggerated expressions and comical interaction. It was like having a live sitcom right in front of me. Honestly, sometimes I would ask a leading question to get them sparring again. "Well, Shauna, how's your love life today?"

"I should have been a bartender or a beauty operator," I used to tell friends who apologized for spilling their tales of woe to me. I was a sympathetic listener. Even in my weakened state, this knack for hearing others tell their stories was appealing.

Most of my bed-bound time was spent staring at the chipped woodwork and black slash marks on the walls. My room was always chilly. I missed the heated blankets given me in the hospital. I couldn't seem to pile on enough of those thin cotton blankets to keep me warm. Television was no company because the overdose of Christmas commercials made me ready to snap.

Christmas came and went without the wonderful Christmas atmosphere I dearly loved. Staring at the poinsettia received from a friend and reading Christmas cards, it still didn't feel like Christmas. Trying to keep our family traditions flowing, Paula called and asked, "Mom, what kind of Christmas cookies can I make for you?" Miles, who had helped my mother and me make lefse for years, ventured out by himself and made the "potato tortilla," as he called lefse, just for me. Christmas was empty for the whole family. Charlie was home alone. Paula was a flight attendant with little time off during the busy holiday season. Miles had moved to Duluth the previous summer to attend graduate school, and was not available. In the past, no matter where we were, our family always came together during the holidays.

Charlie tried to visit as often as possible, but he was, once again, getting weaker and weaker. The last time he visited me at the rehab center, aides had to assist him back to his car. Frail and frightened, he went to the doctor where he was told he needed a heart catheter ablation, a procedure to treat heart arrhythmia—rhythm of the heartbeat.

On New Year's Day, I reflected on the miserable past year. Charlie and I often were alternating hospital stays or in different hospitals at the same time. I believed in God, but He had sure handed us a heavy load. It's said that He doesn't give you more than you can handle; however, during the past year I began to wonder.

Little did I know that bad news would continue to bombard us.

In January, Charlie's foot needed to be amputated due to an infection as the result of diabetes. He was in the hospital. I was at the rehab center. Once again we could not help each other. All we could do was force ourselves to keep calm, listen to each other, and offer emotional support. Although difficult, we even tried to maintain a smidgen of a sense of humor, sharing the few funny events in our lives.

The days confined to a dingy room were numbing. I worked hard to develop my arm strength because I wanted to propel a wheelchair in order to explore my surroundings. Although I still needed help getting out of bed and into the wheelchair, I loved the feeling of independence. In short order, I was on my way: I traveled the halls observing other residents. Watching the birds in the aviary, I wondered why senior communities always have a display of birds. I went to some of the group activities, and while visiting, I learned that often the residents had very interesting histories; they were quite well-educated. I reminded myself, *A frail body does not a frail mind make.*

Initiating conversations, I became a cheerleader for the other men and women who were also struggling with therapy sessions. I challenged a woman well over age 80 to a wheelchair video bowling game. She beat me even though I was a better wheelchair bowler than I ever was as a traditional bowler. I observed that many of the older people would feign sleep when the therapist came to their room to retrieve them. Excuses ranged from, "I have a beauty shop appointment" or "I'm going to bingo now. Maybe later." They did not want to go to therapy. However, I understood how important daily therapy was to my future.

Marion was a blondish-grey, frizzy-haired woman who casually wheeled herself up and down the halls all day. She gave a smooth, beauty queen wave and said "hello" and "good-bye" to everyone she met. Apparently she had been an Aquatennial Queen in her younger days. She did not forget how to do the regal wave to her admiring crowds. I chuckled every time she passed by.

One night I heard a man down the hall continually yelling, "Help, help!" Certain something tragic had happened, I alerted a nurse. She explained that he refused to use the call light. Instead he chose to yell out. It was a little unnerving each time he howled. After a while, no one paid much attention to his outbursts.

On the way to physical therapy, I passed through the section for long-term residents, many with senility or Alzheimer's. One day in the hall, a woman in her wheelchair called out, "Take me to my room. I want to go to my room." When the aide came, she told me that Helen would wheel herself right back into the hall the minute she was returned to her room. Sure enough, on the way back from therapy, she was back in the hall.

Genevieve loved men and tried to flirt with every man she met, young or old. She seemed like a charming older woman, until I heard her in the beauty salon adamantly saying, "No! Leave me alone! I do not want my hair washed." The beauty shop was one of the few luxuries we had. It was not mandatory, so how she got the appointment I can only guess. Maybe a family member thought she was doing her a favor. I saw a different side of sweet, cooperative Genevieve.

As time progressed, I asked the nurses to decrease my pain medication. "I don't think I need it as much as I did and I'm hoping my mind will be less muddled."

I realized if I wanted anything extra, such as ice water or another blanket, I could get it faster if I waited until after three o'clock when the afternoon shift came on duty. They usually didn't have much to do until dinnertime. However, when the next shift changed in the evening around ten, I had no chance of getting anything I might need as they were always short-staffed at night.

If I accidently called a nurse instead of an aide to help me onto the bedpan, the nurse often said, "I'll be right back." That's how I learned nurses don't do bedpans. If they forgot to tell an aide, I was out of luck. Actually, the person who eventually showed up had extra work, because I was most likely already wet and needed a change. If I dropped something on the floor, I had to wait until an aide came in to bring me dinner or check vitals. Then I thought to myself, *I have to remember to ask the aide to get the comb I dropped.* If I didn't, it would be swept out of the room when the cleaning lady came the next morning, unless she missed that spot.

VI

Take Time to Grieve

Now that I was residing more permanently at the rehab center, I savored the frequent visits from friends. At first, friends were hesitant to visit. I am sure they were thinking: *What do we say to a person who has just lost a huge part of her life?* They would bring me books, magazines, homemade treats, and my favorite soda. Mostly, they were relieved I was still the person they knew. We talked. We shared. We laughed. Once they became more comfortable with visiting, they came back often. With laughter came the pleasure of feeling like my old self again, even though I was still not mobile.

Before my collapse, I remember attending a funeral and thinking, *I don't have any friends. No one will come to my funeral.* I regretted not keeping in touch with former neighbors and colleagues. Now I had a circle of precious friends who were closer to me than any previous relationships.

These friends not only visited me but took turns bringing casseroles and homemade soup to Charlie. Not that he would starve on his own, but it's difficult to ask for help. Friends might say, "If you need anything just let me know." How often do we ask for help? Instead our friends said, "Can I stop by with a casserole tonight?" or "I made a batch of homemade cookies. Can I bring them to you?" and "I'm going to the store. Do you need anything while I'm there?" It's easier to get a yes out of these questions. Janine cleaned for us and during this time she took on the extra tasks of washing Charlie's clothes, changing the bed, and she even sealed Christmas card envelopes.

On Valentine's Day, Charlie was planning to visit me. I had made a card for him in an occupational therapy session. The flowers he sent ahead arrived. Charlie did not. He had gotten another infection in his leg, and needed a below-the-knee amputation. Being a fairly composed person, it was hard to tell from his voice the severity of his condition. He'd had many infections in the past, which sometimes made him become delirious. He sounded matter-of-fact; however, I was not by his side to know what was truly going on.

Charlie's second amputation went well. Even with a wheelchair, mobility was difficult for him so the doctors suggested he join me at the rehab center. We were in separate rooms, but delighted to be able to have breakfast, lunch, and dinner together. It had now been four months since we had been able to sit by each other and enjoy our meals.

Together we wheeled ourselves down the long hall to the elevator, going to the lower level where we parked our chairs in the outside patio area and basked in the warm, thawing sunshine. As we sat talking, I daydreamed about wheeling through the parking lot and up to the main street. *Could I handle being in the real world?* It seemed like a daring adventure. Charlie was with me now so I decided not to take any chances. We could stick it out together, though we were both eager to go home.

Taking part in challenging daily therapy, both of us were seeing some recovery, but it was painfully slow.

By March, I didn't know how I would manage when I got home. I was not walking, could stand only for a minute and a half by grasping bars, and still needed assistance turning myself in bed. I relied on the aides operating a transfer device to get me in and out of bed. The Hoyer device was named after one of its manufacturers. The Hoyer served the same purpose as the hammock/swing I had at the Mayo Clinic, except it moved on wheels instead of being hooked to the ceiling. Even though I could not get to the toilet myself, all I wanted was to go home. I was restless and bored gazing out my window at the dirty, melting winter snow, watching the sparrows build a nest under the eaves of the room next door.

Although I begged, still the therapists would not commit to a going-home date. However, the process was accelerated by my insurance company's threats to cut off paying for therapy. Routinely, an occupational therapist accompanies the patient on a home visit. This allows her to evaluate what would be needed for the return to home life.

My excitement was growing; I hadn't been home since November.

The first time I rode the mobility bus I was nervous and anxious, so thankful when I got to the doctor's office that I offered the driver a tip. "In all the years I've worked at this job I've never gotten a tip," he replied. "Well, treat yourself to a cup of coffee," I responded. I couldn't believe how tense my vulnerability had left me. This was only a bus, but, I was not in control of the bus—or myself.

A little less apprehensive the second time I rode the mobility bus, I found myself waiting two hours at the doctor's office for a ride home. A severe snowstorm had slowed traffic to a crawl. I didn't care about the wait. I had a book to read and was out in the *real* world. By this time I had my power chair. Although the chair was large and clumsy, and driven by me, an inexperienced driver, I was still able to successfully maneuver it around in the hospital gift shop. I was cold and hungry when I finally returned to the rehab center. I couldn't wait to tell the aides about my shopping experience. I showed everyone, "Look, I was able to buy my son a birthday card, and how about these cute, comfy red socks?" I wore them with pride, feeling I was returning to normal, mentally at least.

Eagerly I looked forward to my home visit. Passing old familiar landmarks prompted pleasant memories. Everything was still the same. The day was misty, bleak and gloomy as I was maneuvered up the ramp to our condo. I entered rooms darkened by drawn shades. This was not the bright, familiar place I remembered. Boxes of medical supplies were scattered around from Charlie's treatments. The wheels of my wheelchair scrambled the rug in our office. Frustrated, I squealed for the therapist, "I'm trapped. Get me out of here!"

I headed for the kitchen only to find I couldn't get around the kitchen table. We had too many chairs to even get close to the table. If I couldn't stand, I couldn't reach my cupboards. The bathroom was big enough to wheel into, but I took one look at the whirlpool, where I soaked in luxurious bubbles with a good book every Saturday morning, and knew I would never get into that tub again. Frustrated, I thought, *This no longer feels like my home.*

For the first time since I was carted away some five months prior, tears trailed down my cheeks.

VII

Homecoming

Charlie was discharged a couple of weeks before I was, and I desperately wanted to join him. Now my goal was to be home in time to celebrate my son's birthday on April 2. A room needed to be set up for me, with a rented hospital bed and a Hoyer lift. The team of therapists and social workers wanted to arrange full-time care for me. I spoke up, "I sleep well at night. I don't need someone after I go to bed." We agreed on four hours in the morning and in the evening. Even that felt like an intrusion into my personal space. But I had to accept it if I wanted to go home.

Remembering how challenging it was driving my wheelchair on the carpet during my brief home visit, I decided it would be more convenient when moving the Hoyer and manipulating my wheelchair, if the carpet were removed and a laminated floor installed in my bedroom. This idea came to me just three days before I was to be discharged. I called several flooring stores with no success. Then, like fate, I saw the television ad I had seen a million times before: carpeting or laminated floor installation in one day. I thought, *yes, just what I need*. I scheduled the measuring and installation, and it was all in place when I returned home.

"Wow, this is beautiful. I love it," I said to my daughter as I wheeled into the extra bedroom. The room had been painted a bright, sunshiny yellow. My neighbor, who was also my decorator, came to the rehab center and helped me pick out cheerful, flowered fabric for curtains to adorn the window and a matching bedspread. Paula made the bed and put the room together. "Oh, honey, you have made my room look gorgeous. And the fresh flowers—how did you find them to match the curtains?" What a delightful homecoming!

"Mom, I'm just so happy to have you home again," she said, teary-eyed.

Charlie received his prosthesis in April; however, every time he put it on, he would get an infection. That kept him wheelchair-bound for an additional year.

I was totally dependent on others. Fortunately, I had two perfect home health aides: Krista was experienced and extremely capable, while Melinda was kind, gentle, and most obliging. Krista took charge as if she were caring for her own family. She would give me a bed bath, help me get dressed, crank the Hoyer to get me out of bed, and make my breakfast. I would not have my briefs (diapers are for babies, briefs for adults) changed again until she arrived back at six o'clock, at which time she cranked me into and out of bed. This happened every time I had to use the bedpan. Then she made dinner, cleaned up the kitchen, and helped me get ready for bed.

Melinda introduced me to "spa day" on Saturday. This is when she would wash my hair in the kitchen sink, massage my legs, and give me a manicure and pedicure.

In order to use our master bathroom, we had to remove the whirlpool and small shower to make it handicapped-accessible. That meant a new cement floor had to be installed to elevate the shower entrance, making it possible for Charlie and me to roll in on a bath chair. Handrails and an easy-access sink were configured to fit our needs. As with many home-remodeling projects, it became more complicated than we first thought. The bathroom remodel took twice as long as we expected and involved emptying the adjoining closet and replacing shelves and flooring.

All the while Krista and Melinda were trying to find clothes for me to wear that were easy to put on. This meant constantly learning what I could wear, and what I needed to donate. I relinquished rugs, including the one in the office, furniture that had been in the extra bedroom that I now occupied, cookware I could no longer use or reach, and office chairs that both Charlie and I had replaced with our wheelchairs. The aides made many trips to the thrift store with donations. Friends continued to bring Charlie and me dinners and homemade desserts. Our wonderful friends and family looked after us long after we came home.

A physical therapist came to our home three times a week to help develop my strength. Using a flat, smoothly polished board similar to a small surfboard, called a sliding board, I worked on transferring from my wheelchair to the bed and back again. This took all my strength. I was never successful enough to rely on that method. It was not as easy as when you see muscular men pop in and out of their wheelchairs like Lt. Dan Taylor in the movie *Forrest Gump*.

Melancholic and anxious, I thought, *My world has turned upside down. Everything is so difficult. I have to learn simple tasks all over again.* All my plans and dreams of the future had been shattered. It was too depressing to think about what I had lost. I had to concentrate on being as self-sufficient as I could. My path had swerved; I was now on a journey down a new path, albeit a rough and uncharted one.

Diligently I participated in physical therapy, trying anything to become more mobile. I didn't give up. I kept moving forward. No matter how small, I always had a goal. With the weather getting nice, I did not want to be confined to the house. After thinking long and hard, I finally figured it out. If I held the doors open with a rubber-tipped cane, I could motor through without marking the wood doors.

I vividly remember my first solo trip in my power chair. It was a beautiful early summer day. Out the door, down the ramp, across the street, and through the wooded path to the shopping center I went. I felt like Little Red Riding Hood joyfully romping through the woods. As I carefully crossed the street, I heard the traffic noise from the highway a few blocks away, a sound I had never noticed before. Driving along the path, I heard birds, some chirping, some singing. I felt so joyous I even said "hi" to the chipmunk that crossed my path. The wind-blown leaves vibrated in a delightful harmony. I stopped to look at the geese on the pond.

My heart rejoiced in a rebirth and sensitivity to a life I had never felt before.

Home health aides are expensive. In order to receive help from the state for long-term care, sadly, I had to say good-bye to Krista and Melinda.

Looking through pages and pages of home health aide services, I blindly chose a company located nearby. That turned out to be a mistake that led to many traumatic experiences. Often the aides would not show up, leaving me stranded in bed, wet and uncomfortable until another aide was found who could use the Hoyer to get me out of bed, and help me dress. This happened many times. Training new aides several times a week was exhausting. What a hassle! One aide was more dependable, but when she shared several disturbing stories of what she had done to her boyfriend, I became alarmed and did not feel safe with her. I contacted the original company I worked with, and they were kind enough to provide a referral to a more stable company.

VIII

Just Try

Painfully I propped myself up in a chair, sitting there a little longer each day. Fumbling with my reaching device, I patiently picked up every little thing I dropped on the floor. I had to learn to stand if I was to reach the top shelf of my refrigerator. Standing for three minutes was a test of endurance. Being able to get in and out of bed by myself meant I could wheel into the bathroom at night—a great advantage and a wonderful feeling of accomplishment. Each endeavor was a new and challenging experience. Yet each success reinforced my strength, encouraging me to continue.

In July, I began participating in pool therapy at Courage Center, a Minnesota-based non-profit rehabilitation center that prides itself on empowering people with disabilities to realize their full potential. I was excited for two reasons:

First, I had taken water aerobics off and on for fifteen years. "Give me a referral to the Courage Center pool, and I know I will start to walk again," I kept telling my therapist at the rehab center.

Second, while our bathroom was being remodeled, I would be able to take a shower at Courage Center.

As they wheeled me into the pool, the lukewarm water caressed my body. It felt like a warm, fuzzy blanket was wrapping me in comfort and support.

At first my numb legs and feet drifted everywhere, just not where I needed them. They strayed so much I could not tell whether they were positioned right. This left me—and my legs—very unstable; however, I was comfortable in the water. Twice a week I was wheeled into the warm pool for an hour. I focused on sitting and standing; clutching the therapist when I walked just five feet and riding a water noodle to strengthen my core muscles. To do these simple tasks took serious concentration. It was a physical struggle for me.

Gradually I could stand, even walk a little, grasping a pole in each hand. "I'm learning to pole dance," I told Charlie. In order to advance my skills, I needed braces to keep my ankles from turning. Pool therapy continued; and land therapy was added.

Land therapy was exhausting. I never minded walking with the device that looked like a giant baby walker because it meant I was upright and moving. The more arduous the challenge, the harder I struggled to master the task. Hot and sweaty, I'd come back for more—sometimes even gasping out loud, "One step at a time, girl. You can do it!" More sweat. More success. I always disliked exercise that made me sweat, which is why I liked working out in the pool. But I couldn't stop. I practiced standing and sitting, climbing one step, two steps, and then three. I was making some giant strides forward, more than I had ever imagined. I overheard the staff saying, "Look at how well she is doing." By the time I could walk the length of a football field with a walker, stand and sit on my own, and tackle a flight of stairs, I graduated. That was nine months of exhausting therapy two or three days every week. I had surpassed all expectations from doctors, therapists and even myself.

One step just led to another, and it all came together.

IX

Caught in the Middle

While I was going to and from Courage Center for appointments, I depended on the mobility bus. I had overcome my apprehension and was comfortable with this mode of transportation. People with varying degrees of handicaps take this bus. Some people rode the lift with their wheelchairs, as I did. Some grasped walkers. Some gingerly ascended the steps. Others had no visible physical difficulties, but lacked the mental ability to manage mass transit. Even though I might never see the other passengers again, we all shared camaraderie. Some days I made small talk with the driver, or if another passenger wanted to converse, I was a willing participant. I gained new insight into people I might never have met before my paralysis.

One day, as I rode my chair onto the bus, I noticed another woman in the front passenger seat who appeared to be in her late 40's, early

50's. She was a thin, rather wiry woman with short, dark hair and sharp facial features. After my chair was secured and my seatbelt fastened, she asked, "Did you enjoy your pool therapy today?"

"Yes, I always do." I responded. These buses were dreadfully noisy and jarring; everything that wasn't fastened tightly, wiggled and jiggled. I could tell she was used to the bus because she made sure to speak loud enough that I could hear her clearly.

"I had a stroke a year ago," she continued. "I have difficulty moving the left side of my body. I was hospitalized for several months. Later I found out my husband had a girlfriend living at our house while I was gone. Do you think that was right?"

"No," I responded.

"I confronted him with the sex they shared in our bedroom, and he told me he wanted a divorce. Do you think that was right?" Again, I agreed with her. "He turned my boys against me, too," she continued. "Do you think that was right?" I was listening empathetically and didn't feel I needed to respond again. "I had to move in with my sister because he kicked me out of the house."

Starting to feel a little overwhelmed, I was relieved when the bus stopped outside the door of a small, brick warehouse building. Two younger women with no noticeable physical disabilities boarded the bus. Often the bus picks up mentally challenged individuals going to and from work programs. I hoped the addition of these two women would quiet the older woman, and I could ride home somewhat peacefully.

"Why didn't you call me?" the younger woman behind me asked the older woman sitting in the front seat. "You were supposed to call me."

"No, you said you would call me, and I waited."

"I never said I would call you."

"Yes, you did. I remember you telling me you would call me."

The tone of the conversation was escalating. Each was annoyed with the other for not making the first telephone call. I felt like the net in a volleyball game. It was quiet for a few minutes. Then it started again. Both accused the other of not making the first call.

Ladies, ladies, does it really matter? I'm thinking to myself, afraid to enter this war of words. Quiet again. Then back at it with the same accusations. I noticed the other younger woman in the left front seat was totally oblivious to what was going on. It occurred to me that she might have witnessed this same interaction between these two women on previous rides.

Finally, after they had exhausted their accusations, the older lady said, "Well, I will call you tomorrow."

I thought to myself, *Finally it ends.*

The younger woman responded, "You didn't call me last time. How do I know you will call me this time?"

"You were supposed to call me," and it started once again. It was like two children fighting over the shovel in a sandbox: Neither was willing to let go of the issue.

The bus stopped. The younger woman prepared to exit. As she walked down the steps she warned, "You better call me this time."

What a relief to hear only the familiar sound of the bus bumping and rattling.

X

Overcoming Challenges

As an only child, I was praised, rewarded, and told I could tackle anything. Maybe that's why I have fairly solid self-confidence. Maybe it's just my nature to gravitate to a challenge.

Even as a child, boundaries never hindered my curiosity. I never saw fences, just open fields. I was not gifted with a natural talent for academics, arts, sports, music, dance or skillfulness. Still I was always determined to try.

"Do you want to take modeling lessons?" my mother asked. "Oh, that would be fun." When the agency called me, it seemed I was most often a little too chubby to be considered. Mom didn't give up, "How would you like to take tap and ballet dancing?"

"A dancer? Yes." A few recitals later, we knew I wasn't cut out for the dance stage.

Knowing I definitely did not have a voice, this time mom said, "MacPhail School of Music offers drama lessons. You'd be good at that." Mom's confidence in me made me believe it myself. She said, "You can do it," and I did. *Just try*, I thought to myself. *Mom says I can do it.*

The prize was not my reward.
The challenge was what lit my fire.

I remember reading to my children the Rudyard Kipling book, *Rikki-Tikki-Tavi,* about the snake and the mongoose. I related to the mongoose that demonstrated persistence, patience, and tenacity in capturing the snake. Although patience is not the strongest of these traits, I learned a great deal of patience while dealing with my disability. Patience is a beautiful art.

My journey began by accepting that I would never walk again. As with those suffering from addictions, I first had to acknowledge my condition. I didn't dwell on what I didn't have. Instead, I concentrated on what I did have: determination. I was being trained to work within my limitations. I had to conquer my obstacles.

Now I was experiencing more than the doctors or I had ever imagined possible. I was stepping outside of my given limitations.

When he heard of my success, my doctor at the Mayo Clinic responded with a confirming letter that read, "I am certainly happy to hear how you are doing. The improvement, from the time when you were the weakest, is quite amazing. I am sure that a lot of your improvement has come from simply not giving up hope and being determined to get better."

"Whatever you do you need courage,
whatever course you decide upon,
there is always someone
to tell you that you are wrong.
There are always difficulties arising
that tempt you to believe
your critics are right.
To map out a course of action
and follow it to the end
requires some of the same courage
that a soldier needs. Peace has its victories,
but it takes brave men and women
to win them."
Ralph Waldo Emerson

To be honest, I must admit the progress I made was not fueled merely by self-motivation. Courage is deciding there is something more important. Between 2008 and 2009, God challenged Charlie and me with serious health deterioration. He also gave us the strength and courage to move beyond our handicaps. Then, during the second half of 2009, He blessed us with an exceptionally wonderful year with many of my dreams coming true.

After thirty-seven years of waiting, Paula married Chris, the same man who told me on that critical day in the hospital that he would always be there for her. They moved into a house filled with challenges: a sunken living room and circular stairs. Most exciting, they were expecting my first grandchild by the end of the year.

I had to surmount the obstacles. Both Charlie and I were confined to wheelchairs for her wedding. That didn't stop us from being elated and as jubilant as kindergarteners on their first day of school. I even swung my chair around on the dance floor. To go to the bathroom at my daughter's house required a new talent, for she had no railings to grasp. I had to be strong enough to sit and stand to use their lower toilet. To get around in their home, I had to learn to climb up and down stairs. And how would I manage taking care of a new baby? I was motivated by challenges.

Six years earlier, before the medical storm ravaged our lives, Charlie and I had moved into our condo. Whenever we drove by Oak Knoll Lutheran Church on the corner, one of us would say, "We need to try that church some time."

Our dear friend, Pat, asked if her college friend, Linda, who was a member of Oak Knoll, would contact the pastor to visit us. Pastor Paul Pettersen visited us twice at the rehab center. We both felt very comfortable with him. Having managed to get through the condo doors on my own using my motorized chair, one Sunday I decided to travel two blocks to the church.

A little embarrassed at first, I drove my clunky power chair into the vestibule. Everyone was extremely welcoming. At first I tried to discreetly hide at the back of the church, feeling like the proverbial bull in a china shop. After a few Sundays, I lingered in the sanctuary until everyone had left. I practiced driving my chair up to the altar to see if I would be able to take communion with the other parishioners. YES!

Next, when I advanced to a walker, I parked my chair outside the chapel and did a practice run again to see if I could manipulate the aisle and pews.

Every Sunday, providing it didn't rain, I put my chair in third gear and headed for church. The sun shone through the plethora of colors nestled in the stained-glass windows. The choir, the musician with the guitar, the bell choir, and the inspirational messages from

Pastor Paul and Pastor Michelle Abbott kept me coming back for more.

Charlie was more hesitant to become churched. After making it clear to Pastor Paul that he had a lot of reservations about religion, Pastor told him he was welcome to join anyway. The fall of 2009 Charlie and I joined the church.

When Charlie started attending church, we both took the mobility bus two blocks just to get there. He started going to the front of the church for communion in his wheelchair. As I moved on to a cane and he to a walker, fellow parishioners would stop us on the way out and say, "I can't believe it when I see the two of you walking up to the front. It's a miracle."

"Yes, it sure seems like a miracle," I responded. Charlie was not sure what happened either. He just knew that ever since he joined the church, he hadn't had a single health problem.

Two years after I first collapsed, I was walking with a walker, grasping the railing to climb stairs, standing to get my own glass of milk, putting dishes in the microwave above the stove, fixing a meal, showering, and even driving a car. Charlie didn't drive, although he was nearly as mobile as I was.

No, I'm not the same as I was three years ago. I miss the wind in my hair when I see a bicyclist whizzing by. I am uncomfortable babysitting my granddaughter alone. Nevertheless, together Charlie and I can handle even a toddler and do a good job of spoiling her. I have some neuropathy, a loss of nerve sensation, from my waist to my toes. But I feel healthy and am still challenging myself. My granddaughter, Olivia, is walking now, and I can follow her using a cane. She and I learned to walk together. One day I saw her with a stick in her hand holding it like a cane. As we walked down the hall, we looked like two little old ladies. We swim together. I can even hold her if I am standing up against a wall. I can be a *real* grandmother—a dream comes true.

When I accepted my limitations,
I let go of the past.
I saw only the future,
and each small step inched me
closer to my former self.

Learning to walk again did not come easy. Every day I walked and climbed stairs to strengthen my legs. It was grueling work. I still conscientiously do my morning bed exercises and participate in pool therapy twice a week to keep up my stamina.

By August of 2010 I was walking fairly well and was convinced I could drive a car. It had been nearly two years since I drove. *Was it like riding a bicycle—you never forget once you have learned?* Aware of my tendency to jump in the pool, then find out if there was water in it, I thought I should take the driving assessment offered at Courage Center before I took to the streets. With the instructor on the passenger side I gingerly got behind the wheel. I was struck with a moment of panic. I wasn't familiar with this brand of car and felt I might have bitten off more than I could chew. "Okay, we're ready to go. I'll give you directions when to turn," said the instructor.

It's now or never, I thought to myself. Cautiously I drove out of the garage, heading for the street. I made a left turn here, a right turn there, onto the highway, and into the shopping center for a parking exercise, all the while focusing on where the gas pedal was in relation to the brake. After an hour I drove the car back into the Courage Center garage. I had passed the test. The instructor said it might be wise for me to stick close to home at first. I wasn't as self-assured as when I had started, but I knew with practice it would come. And it all came back to me—just like riding a bike.

In June of 2011, Charlie and I went on an Alaskan cruise. As expected, it wasn't as easy as on past cruises: neither of us had the same physical strengths and abilities. Nevertheless, breathing the fresh, cool air reminded us how far we had come and how lucky we were to be alive. Alaska is truly God's country—and we are all God's children.

Three years ago several doctors told me I would never walk again. Certainly, I'd never travel. It's amazing, once you let go, you are free to forge ahead—often more than you or anyone could envision.

Although I worked hard, I do not believe I did it all myself. God threw his safety net out to me and kept me on a steady path. He had healed my spine enough so now I can walk. If He had not given me the opportunity to walk again, I would still know that He cared about me and gave me strength to move forward.

"He stilled the storm to a whisper;
the waves of the sea were hushed."
Psalm 107:29 (NIV)

Friends tell me they are inspired by my recovery. I am amazed by my improvement. The Hoyer lift I had rented to help me out of bed has been returned. The power chair I had wanted so I would not be confined at home, is now used only for long jaunts, or when sitting at my computer. I use a walker or a cane, even drive. The ramp Paula and Chris had purchased for me to use to roll into their sunken living room, is now packed away.

Once again, I am in charge of my life. I prepared for the worst, and I got the best. I am incredibly thankful that God gave me the determination to rise above my disability and move forward. I have increased awareness of the world around me and appreciate every step I take.

> *"God's love frees me to take risks,*
> *to surprise even myself with courage,*
> *sometimes to fall flat on my face*
> *but always to move onward*
> *with the knowledge that*
> *God is encouraging me."*
> Christian Affirmation of Faith

Years ago I worked at a company housed in an older building. The radiator rattled intermittently. The clamor was persistent and disturbing. One day, men fixed the radiator. It was quiet, like a normal radiator, but when they removed the pain of the noise, the quiet seemed like a gift.

In an interview with Oprah Winfrey, J.K. Rowling, author of the Harry Potter series, admitted, "Rock bottom became the foundation of my life." When you are down and out, as she was before she became a successful writer, you don't have anything to lose from trying.

Accepting where you are is the first step to climbing out.

When we think we can no longer go on, or the road ahead has been washed away, we can listen to the words of Quinn Redlin Kintner, who wrote the following poem before she died at age twenty. She had cerebral palsy, was completely deaf, and unable to say a word. Still this bright, young woman, who communicated with sign language and by computer, had a full life. She is an inspiration to us all. Quinn wrote:

I am a person of infinite possibility.
I have known that as long as I can remember.

The textures of my life
tell of my possibilities.
I am rough with scars and uncertainty.
I am torn from thoughts and ideas.
I am colored by experience and dreams.
I am cut from what I know and learn.
I am shiny with care and polish.
I am worn from time.
I am wet with tears.
I am floating on laughter

I am a person of infinite possibility.
I know that.

At Courage Center I see a multitude of people with varying degrees of immobility and pain. I am inspired by each and every one, simply because they are striving to accomplish their potential. Just by taking part in therapy sessions, working out in the accessible gym, or exercising in the pool, they are reaching out to better themselves.

In my quiet times, I wonder, *What does the future have in store for me? What other challenges will I have to overcome the stronger I get?*

I am ready to tackle whatever comes my way.

> *"I can do everything through*
> *Him who strengthens me."*
> Philippians 4:13 (NIV)

Epilogue

These past three years Charlie and I have been on a horrendous, yet amazing, voyage. We now have a fairly normal routine, and both of us are grateful to be home. My sunshiny bedroom has turned into our granddaughter, Olivia's, room when she visits. She will soon share the room with a baby sister. Nothing is more treasured than my granddaughter greeting me with a leaping hug and a sloppy kiss. I anticipate cradling her newborn sister as she drifts off into a peaceful sleep, and watch with pride as Paula and Chris lovingly parent my granddaughters, and admire Miles' adoration for his niece.

Sometimes when I am having a little pity party, I wish I didn't have to use a cane or a walker to get around. My ego thinks it makes me look older. Then I stop and say to myself, *Look where you came from, paralysis. Now you are walking. How lucky you are. Be thankful.*

How can you lament a journey that makes you stronger, both mentally and physically?

Yes, I am truly blessed for the miracle I experienced. It took courage and determination—no more than any of us can muster if we try. Will we succeed? Not always. But if it's important we need to try.

None of us knows what the future holds. However, I do know that whatever it is, my family, friends and most importantly, God, will be with me.

"The future is called 'perhaps,'
which is the only possible thing
to call the future. And the only
important thing is not to allow
that to scare you."
-Tennessee Williams, *Orpheus Descending*, 1957

Olivia perched on the arm of Kathi and Charlie's wheelchairs. December 2010

CPSIA information can be obtained at www.ICGtesting.com
Printed in the USA
BVOW010421301111

277206BV00001B/1/P